SANTA MARIA PUBLIC LIBRARY

CO-DBG-620

A Mother's Thoughts in Verse

By Henrietta Cassady

SANTA MARIA PUBLIC LIBRARY

PublishAmerica
Baltimore

© 2005 by Henrietta Cassady.
All rights reserved. No part of this book may be reproduced, stored in a retrieval system or transmitted in any form or by any means without the prior written permission of the publishers, except by a reviewer who may quote brief passages in a review to be printed in a newspaper, magazine or journal.

First printing

At the specific preference of the author, PublishAmerica allowed this work to remain exactly as the author intended, verbatim, without editorial input.

ISBN: 1-4241-0562-5
PUBLISHED BY PUBLISHAMERICA, LLLP
www.publishamerica.com
Baltimore

Printed in the United States of America

I would like to dedicate this book to my daughter Melissa for all her help.

Family

Austin

I have a very special friend
And Austin is his name.
Every time that I see him
Austin is always the same.
He has the biggest prettiest smile
He has to travel many miles.
Loves his mom and dad a lot
Austin likes it when it's hot.
He'll be six when his birthday comes around
Maybe the circus will come to his town.
Libby is the name of his sister
I bet she is a little blister.
They have fun when they play
Close to each other they will stay.
Austin is going thru a hard thing
Yet he sits around and sings.
My prayer for him is to be ok
So I'll thank God and daily pray.
To take care of this special little boy
Who brings to his family so much joy.

5-17-2005

A Family

God made the first family Adam and Eve.
The devil slithered in and began to deceive.
God placed them in a very beautiful garden.
Made coats of skin and their sin he did pardon
All families are created from heaven above
They are given to us to care for and to love
No home is a family without God at the head.
He sees and hears all that is done and said.
God put all families with each other.
Some with sisters and some with a brother
No matter what family God put you in.
Always love them and treat them as a friend.
Be there for them to the very end.
Let them know on you they can depend
When you get saved you're in the family of God.
A different life you live and new paths you trod.
Our heavenly family has a heavenly home
Where we will live and never more roam.

11-13-03

A Son

A son is a gift from God above.
He is given to his family to love.
A son is a son wherever he may go.
Whether his love for you does show.
He will brighten your life each day.
By some action or thing he may say.
A wise son makes a glad father.
Don't make him feel, he is a bother.
Be considerate of his feelings each day.
Then you will have a son to stay.
When a son always obeys God's ways,
He'll have a friend and length of days.
Long ago God gave us his only Son.
To save our souls and give us a home.
Still millions disobey and try to run.
From that Son and what He has done.
So you be a son God will welcome there.
To that home we're told he has prepared.

7-22-04

Birthday Girl

Once upon a time in a little town.
A baby girl was born who wasn't allowed to run around.
She grew up into a beautiful girl.
But never did she give the boys a twirl.
Then one day she left our little town.
And all she did was run around.
She fell in love one certain day.
Now at home she has to stay.
Now the years have come and gone.
She only goes out to give the dog a bone.
Today is her birthday, I must say
Maybe someone will come and take her away.
My wish for her for the coming years,
Is to run around and a lot less tears.

1-29-2003

Blake

I have a grandchild named Blake.
A million dollars for her, I wouldn't take.
She is the apple of her Granny's eye.
I sing to her of songs on high.
Blake sure does love her big sister.
But sometimes she acts like a little blister.
She loves to pull Tyanna's hair.
I think the two of them are quite a pair.
She likes to eat with the radio on.
Cuts it on and off as we go along.
She is Mommy's pretty little girl.
With great big blue eyes, and lots of curls.

1-13-98

Brothers

God gives us brothers from above.
To have, to hold and always to love.
Brothers are special to us all.
Always ready to help us if we fall.
They will protect you along the way
So listen carefully to what they say.
You can depend on a brother all of the time.
Whether he is rich or only has a dime.
Be good to your brother as God would have you to do
Then you'll have a friend that will remain true.
A brother can be a very special friend.
He will always love you to the very end.

3-31-04

Bye O

Chorus:
Bye O, Bye O, Bye O, my pretty baby,
Bye O, my pretty baby, Bye O
Bye O, Bye O, Bye O, my pretty baby,
Bye O, my pretty baby, Bye O

Granny loves you so, more than you could ever know
Bye O, My pretty girl Bye O.
I love you with all my heart and soul.
Bye O, My pretty girl Bye O.

Now close your eyes and go to sleep
Bye O, My pretty girl Bye O.
And don't you make one single peep.
Bye O, My pretty girl Bye O.

10-01-96

Children

Children are the little people on the earth.
They come kicking and screaming at their birth.
We feed them on formula and baby food.
Then sit around and listen to them coo.
Soon they learn to crawl and walk.
Jabber all the time and try to talk.
They love to run and play all day.
Want you to listen to all they say.
Children like for us to read to them.
While some like for us to sing hymns.
They fill our lives with so much fun.
And always keep us on the run.
God gives us children from above.
To take care of, to teach and love.
So try not to let them get on your nerves.
Instead be a friend and try to serve.
What a treasure God gives to us.
We can take them to church on the bus.
They are dependent on you and me.
So please hug and sit them on your knee.
Remember, you were a child one day.
Then try to listen to what they say.

8-6-98

Curt

One day a boy named Curt came around.
With my daughter he could be found.
He didn't talk very much those days.
Had an old pickup and some funny ways.
At first he lived with his mother.
He has one sister and no brothers.
Time went on Curt moved in with his Dad.
Now he lives upstairs in his new pad.
Days went by Curt made Melissa his bride.
I went to the wedding and how I cried.
He has now a wife and two little girls.
One with straight hair and the other with curls.
Never put the drainers in the sink
It will pluck his nerves and make you think.
He sure does enjoy his little fishes.
When the holidays come he has lots of wishes.
Curt loves his music as you can see.
Has several tapes and lots of CDs.
Playing on the computer is fun for him.
He gets upset if you take his pens.
Travels down the road now to Ultra-Prise.
Everyday now for him is a big surprise.
He is my son-in law as you guessed.
So I'll be quiet and let him tell you the rest.

5-22-99

Dakota

Dakota is Granny's pretty girl,
With lots of hair but not any curls.
Her Daddy named her after a truck,
So I guess with her we're stuck.
Her mother teaches her dirty dancing.
Too and fro you'll see her prancing.
She's not allowed to drink any soda,
So you see why we call her Dakota.
She loves to crawl all over the floor,
Back and forth to the air conditioner cord.
Dakota's favorite past time is her swinging,
While listening to her Granny's singing.

8-29-96

Dear Brother

I have prayed for you for years
Have cried and there has been many tears.
Are there any sins in your life worth keeping?
For one day you'll have a terrible reaping.
It breaks my heart for your soul to be lost
When Jesus paid for your sin at an awful cost.
Why would you reject his love given so free?
Just repent of all your sins on bended knee.
You'll have peace in your heart like none other
Become a member of Gods family with sisters and brothers.
Please don't put it off until it is too late
Because you will not ever enter Heaven's gates.

5-17-2005

Devyn

Sweetest boy this side of Heaven,
God gave Devyn to his Granny,
So she could tan his little fanny.
But he is just ole so sweet,
So Granny only has to pinch his cheek.
He usually follows Granny around,
When she visits our big town.
Devyn has friends, named Pam and Randy,
That's where he goes when he wants to get sandy.
A happy little boy playing with his toys,
Especially with the girls and boys.
But the sweetest Devyn can be,
Is when he is sitting on his Granny's knee.

8-29-96

Dreama

I had always longed and prayed for a baby.
Then one day I thought well maybe.
I went to the doctors and to my surprise,
I was going to have a baby with big blue eyes.
In the course of time my baby was born.
I was so happy I felt like blowing a horn.
She didn't care much about playing with her toys.
But when she grew up was popular with the boys.
When Dreama was in school she loved to sell things,
At church, around the neighborhood, she could be seen.
Dreama got married which was a little scary.
She brought home this guy which was so hairy.
Has two children named Devyn and Dakota.
Now she sits around drinking her soda.
Dreama now works at Kerch's Ribs & Chicken.
Watching the people sitting there licking.
At camp Dreama's special friend was Mike.
They goofed and horsed around half the night.
Now this is the end of my little tale.
If you listen carefully you'll hear her wail.

1-14-98

Henrietta

In the mountains of West Virginia a girl was born.
When growing up she loved to eat birch and corn.
Loved to play out there at the corncrib.
Woman was first made from a man's rib.
She has seven brothers and three sisters.
When younger she sure was a little blister.
Was always into the warming closet for scrappies.
Put a smile on her face and made her happy.
One of her favorite things was going to school.
She played in the river, but had no pool.
Almost all her family lives faraway.
Her heart yearns to see them everyday.
Henrietta got married when almost twenty-five.
Had two girls and one boy by her side.
She enjoys going to church with all her friends.
No matter what she needs on them she can depend.
Has always loved doing things for others.
How I thank God for all those brothers.
Past time is to sing and do her word search.
Loves to teach the children at her church.
Now Henrietta lives alone on Greenside.
Sometimes she liked to runaway and hide.
But her children and grandchildren are her life.
They fill her days with lots of joy and strife.
She has a sense of humor as you can plainly see.
Is always doing something and is busy as a bee.

8-20-98

Melissa

My second daughter I named Melissa Ann.
If anything was to be done she said I can.
When she was little she couldn't carry a tune.
I told her I'd pray she'd be able to sing soon.
Now time has passed she sings for Miss Perry.
Always around the school, she's in a hurry.
When growing up she was terrible at cooking.
I think because she wasn't even looking.
Melissa when younger liked playing with her toys.
But when a teenager, became interested in the boys.
She almost broke her poor mother's heart.
I said Melissa these boys have got to part.
When upset she'd sing in her room, I want my freedom.
She'd play that screaming meamie, and I'd want my freedom.
Melissa went to work for Merle at Subway.
She said girl you gotta get out of here someway.
So she went out and got a job at Citicorp.
Making those big bucks out near the airport.
Now time has passed and she works at First Data.
Making the people around her a little sadder.
She still doesn't know too much about cooking.
But Curt, Tyanna, and Blake keep her booking.

1-14-98

Memories

When you return to your childhood home.
What will you find that you left behind?
Maybe there will be nothing there to find.
Just your childhood books and a dirty comb.
Will there be cards from places you did roam?
Memories come flooding thru your mind.
A childhood family and the love you shared.
You miss them so much every day.
If only there could have been some other way.
In your heart you know God knows best.
Because His love excels all the rest.
So when it's your time to leave.
Where will you go? What will you leave behind?
A testimony for God and Heaven in mind.

7-17-04

Mother

She came wrapped in beauty.
To do God's will was her duty.
No one else can take her place.
She is important to the human race.
God has first place in her heart.
And to teach her children from the start.
On earth her love excels all others.
She is thankful God made mothers.
She teaches her children to honor and obey.
God's word teaches it even today.
Spends hours weeping and praying for you
That you'd live for God and remain true.
She tries to protect you from all harm.
And then lovingly wraps you in her arm.
She never seeks or desires her own.
Her goal is to make a happy home.
A good name is rather to be chosen,
Than great riches. This is mother.

5-5-99

Mother

A good mother is always kind.
Her children are always on her mind.
Her joy is to take good care of them
On her they will forever depend.
To pray for them is her daily task.
She goes to her Father and continually asks,
To make them children of God.
To guide where their feet may trod.
When no longer home, they are missed
She anxiously awaits their next kiss.
She is happy when grandchildren come
She wishes every good mother to have some.
Now she'll train them in God's way
And pray close by him, they'll always stay.

5-08-05

My Brothers

When growing up I had the privilege of having seven brothers.
They were all the offspring of my Father and my Mother.
Feeding the chickens and milking the cows was never a chore.
But playing blind man together, sometimes was a bore.
They always helped their sisters make corn stalk and acorn men.
Even helped to create that polk berry ink for their fountain pen.
Our brother Carl created a beautiful mud house one-day.
Someone knocked it down; you should have heard me pray.
When working in the fields, he loved to drink his sweet milk.
But when he was stingy with his popcorn, he wasn't wearing silk.
Emmett went rolling down the river in a boat over the ridge.
They all loved the scare their sisters on the swinging bridge.
My brothers helped daddy cut logs and slop the hogs at home.
He tried to teach them good values and never more roam.
Wesley and Russell had a bullhorn to keep in touch with each
other.
He'd walk around rolling his eye's back in his head and say Oh
brother.
Harless liked standing at the road selling chinquapins for 25
cents a glass.
While Russel loved chasing those Cooper girls, trying to make a
pass.
James was afraid of the turkey gobbler, but he would argue with
a fence post.
But Harless loved to whistle and whum more than anyone on
the coast.
He would ride Old Sam to the store to get the corn mealed.
Everywhere he went, the people's eyes were pealed.
Favorite pastime was singing "The Old Country Church" while
carrying water from the spring.

Knowing all the fun their sisters would have when all those fish they cleaned.
I don't think any of us sisters liked to iron our brother's pants.
Anymore than we liked those pesky little red ants.
So through the years and tears, I thank God for my brothers.
If I had to choose my family I would not want any other.

1-21-98

My Sisters

I have three sisters as everybody should know.
We always played together in sunshine and the snow.
In the mountain of West Virginia we were all born.
If you came by, you could see one of us shelling corn.
The first of us sisters to enter the world was Willa Mae,
When she spoke we had to listen to what she had to say.
She's the only one of us who doesn't know how to climb a tree.
I don't know if she's afraid she'll fall and hurt her little knee.
Lelia and Pina loved to go wading in the creek.
They would always sneak off to the water once a week.
Catching those crawdads was always a chore.
But there is one thing about it, it was never a bore.
The light in our eyes was that of our Mother.
If we searched the world over, we'd want no other.
You may ask what makes your sisters so unique.
It's because we love each other everyday of the week.
Growing up one of our favorite foods were those good ole salad greens.
Picking them all over the fields we sisters could be seen.
Mom taught us sisters to enjoy it when we cook.
I know if we tried hard, we could even write a book.
God made us all different as you can plainly see.
He gave us talents and made us special as can be.
So if you have a sister, love and appreciate her in every way.
And thank God in Heaven he gave them to you on that special day.
Now time has passed and we all live miles apart.
But we still love each other from the depths of our heart.

Sisters

What is a sister, you may say.
Someone you see most every day.
But when older they are seldom seen.
When growing up, it's the natural thing
You can talk to a sister as none other.
She will be as close as your mother.
She is one on whom you can depend.
And if your try hard a very close friend.
A sister loves you at all times.
You are continually on her mind.
A sister will always remain true.
She is happy at the thought of you.
Happy memories go flying through her mind.
When in her thoughts, she seems to find.
Some little thing she's come to loves so much.
Could easily vanish away with one little touch.
A sister will always be a part of you.
Whenever you go or whatever you do.
She may not show or tell you all the time.
You're in her heart and forever on her mind.
If you have a sister, Thank God up above.
That he counted you worthy to have such love.

3-5-04

Tyanna

Tyanna can't play a piano.
Tho' she is Granny's first grandchild,
For her I'd walk or run a mile.
She is the light in her mother's eyes.
As bright and blue as the pretty sky.
What makes Tyanna really happy,
Is when she's beating up her Pappy.
Granny calls her, her bugaloo.
One day I'll take her to the zoo.
She always wants to play beauty shop.
Sometimes I think she'll never stop.
She always wraps up in a towel.
So that is why she is her mother's pumpkin pal.

8-29-96

Victor

My third child was a boy I named Victor.
Sometimes other people called him Hector.
He was called four eyes peeping thru the glass.
Playing with matchbox cars, and making ruts in the grass
His best friends were Kirk and Frank.
Everyday one of them needed spanked.
Victor loves to ride his bicycle all over the place
But he worried his mother because he liked to race.
He mowed grass fro a woman named Geraldine.
Now the he's married she's seldom seen.
Victor loved to drive his mothers Toyota truck.
But one way or another he was always stuck.
We always went to 7- Eleven for late night treats
Even though his mother was always beat.
He'd bring his friends to mom's work at Subway
And they would bum food some of the days.
Victor was always in trouble at school
But there is one thing about it, he was nobody's fool.

1-14-98

Friends

Friends

A friend loves you at all times.
Whether you're rich or have a dime.
Willing always to come to your aid.
I've never heard of none being paid.
Cheers you when you're feeling down.
Comfort when none can be found.
Someone to tell your troubles to.
When you are lonely and feeling blue.
A person who goes the extra mile,
And will help you through every trial.
A friend sticks closer than a brother.
Will be there for you like your mother.
Many hours with them you will spend.
As the days go by on them you'll depend.
If you have friends, thank God above.
That in his mercy, he showed such love.

5-11-99

Friendship

Friends are like flowers in the garden of life.
You cultivate and water without any strife.
They take a lot of special nourishment to grow.
But you'll reap many blessings as you sow.
They are planted there by God's guiding hand.
Built on the rock and not on the sand.

3-31-01

Charles Fox

Charles Fox is my son in-laws father
Helping others is a delight not a bother.
He has a gray beard and gray hair
Also has false teeth but will not wear.
Loves for Nancy to fix his favorite meals
If he could, I know he would kick up his heels.
He has one girl and only one boy
Doesn't live far from his brother Roy.
Works in Martinsburg for Waste Management people
Picks up lots of garbage and has seen many steeples.
He comes dirty from work most days
Would be happy if they gave him a big raise.
Sometimes on Saturdays he will haul metal
Gets into his yellow truck and puts his foot to the pedal.
Charles likes to watch NASCAR racing on TV
His dog Hootie will sit at his knee.
He likes to collect those little John Deere tractors
Sings bass in choir at church but he's no actor.
The Baltimore Orioles is his favorite team
To go see them play is one of his dreams.
Most people will say Charles is a nice man
If you need help, he will gladly lend a hand.
His job is necessary for all near or far
If not, garbage would pile up to the very stars.

5-6-2005

Class of 1960

We all went to school in Mercer County
But I doubt any dried their clothes in Downy.
Our school bus driver was Henry Karnes
We saw many things and lots of barns.
He used to call our bus a Cracker Jack box
But he never ran over any fox.
Mrs. Gleason taught the students in Music class
It was so much fun to sing and try to pass.
When we had our concerts, it was a lot of fun
We rode the bus and to Bluefield we would run.
We had very good teachers, when in school
They taught us what we needed, and to obey the rule.
Mr. Farley was the best History teacher around
Taught us the Gettysburg Address and not to make a sound.
In library, I wanted to know how each book turned out
I'd always read the last page and sometimes pout.
In school Emerson was called very smart
From friends or homework, he would not part.
There were some who enjoyed picking on you
They made you mad, sad and a little blue.
But they have changed now as you can see
For they keep themselves busy as a bee.
We are going to have a reunion in July
Some of us will be sure to cry.
It's nice to see friends of years gone by
I hope it won't be a cloudy sky.
We'll all set and talk of years of old
Will be a delight to hear the stories that are told.
We had forty-four to graduate in our year
But two have passed away and we shed tears
We're very blessed no more of us are gone.
For God in his mercy, left us with a song.

5-30-2005

Dan

One day at church I met a man named Dan.
If anything was to be done he said I can.
He has many talents as everyone can see
Because every time you see him, he's busy as a bee.
He cuts his own hair, which I know is a chore.
Not in my lifetime have I seen it done before.
I've never seen anyone have so many keys.
How he remembers where they all go is beyond me.
Dan can always find use for those discarded things.
When I watch him, how it makes my heart sing.
He loves to come home to his bumblebee tuna.
And have his mouthwatering enjoyment real soona.
He always takes us for tours around the church.
Checking to see if things are ok and anyone is a lurch.
He never complains about driving me around.
To church or the doctor wherever I am found.
So you see, this man Dan comes in handy.
If you are real nice, he may give you candy.

1-18-98

Elizabeth

Elizabeth is one of my pen pals.
I'm sitting here writing to her now.
She's a little girl that's awful giggly.
When she sets in church she's wiggly.
But she is still my little friend.
Maybe someday I'll buy her a pen.
This girl is so loving and kind.
A true jewel, and one of a kind.
She loves to sing and play in the snow.
And is very smart as everyone knows.
When she grows up, may be a teacher.
For sure, she won't be a woman preacher.
Don't let her have too many sweets.
She'll have you laughing off your feet.
She can read good for a girl of her age.
You ought to see her flip the page.
Her hairdos take my breath away.
She's one of a kind that's all I can say.

1-30-98

Ethel

I have a new friend at church named Ethel.
When I think about her, I think of going to Bethel.
She tells us all her eyesight isn't very well.
But God still delivered her soul from hell.
Ethel sure does love children as anyone can see.
I know she'd love to bounce a couple on her knee.
She is always willing to work, when things need to be done.
I guess she'd stay and help till the rising sun.
Her home is downtown at The Potomac Towers.
She's way up high but has no garden for flowers.
I guess her favorite pastime is riding the Commuter Bus.
One place, or the other, she's always in a rush.
Ethel has a sweet tooth as everybody knows.
But if you took a hard look at her it doesn't show.
So what do I think of my new friend.
I think she is a sweet person on whom I can depend.

1-15-98

Evelyn

Evelyn is a friend in town
You hardly see her spirits down
Lived in Hagerstown for a long time
I have friends and she is mine
Her brothers and sisters don't live near
But to her they are very dear
People know her all around town
Where her presence can be found
We've missed her at church for so long
But is sick and has to stay home.
My prayer for her is to be back soon
Then we will sing her a welcome tune
Her place is empty in the room
Maybe she will be back soon.
She is always concerned about her friends.
She is someone on whom we can depend
We miss her bright and cheery face.
For you see, No one else can take her place.

11-11-03

Faith

Faith is a little girl that I love
She likes to learn about God above.
She has curly hair and brown eyes
At her grandma's she likes the pies.
Likes you to read to her, while sitting on your lap
She is so interested. She never takes a nap.
She is a smart little girl, for her age
She makes me laugh when I turn the page.
Likes her fruit snacks and her candy
She gets along just fine and dandy.
She'll share with you, if you ask
For her it's not a very hard task.
She makes the cutest little faces
Is seen in a lot of different places.
Her parents nicknamed her Foo Foo.
For she will always be special to them too.

5-23-05

Florence

I've known a woman named Florence for many years.
We have been friends together through heartache and tears.
I was told she had been married several times.
When it comes to men, she couldn't make up her mind.
Scattered over a couple of states, she has children and grandchildren.
They help to fill her life and mind each day.
Now she can only dream of men, but to be married no way.
She still loves to go to the riverbank fishing.
I sure hope one of these days she don't come up missing.
Florence used to crochet footies for all her friends.
Now all she does is lay around with people who use Depends.
She lives at Colton Villa at the ripe old age of eighty-seven.
Who knows before long she'll be walking the streets of Heaven.
She is my friend on whom I can depend.
So I guess we will be friends to the very end.

7-22-98

Grace

I know a little girl named Grace.
She sure does go at a fast pace.
She is such a pretty little girl
I've seen her stand and twirl and twirl.
She loves her grandma as you can see
She makes her happy as can be.
Has three sisters and no brothers
If she could choose she'd want none other.
To Sunday school and church she will go
Her family all sits in just one row.
She sings for the people at Avalon
They all smile, for her they're fond.
She loves for you to read her books
You have all her attention as she looks.
She is different in so many ways
But a sweet little girl, I hope she stays.

5-24-05

Jimmy

A few years ago when I worked at Subway.
A cute curly haired man came in one day.
I learned he was the owner of Kerches Ribs and Chicken.
He has some employee's there who are always kickin'
I hear Jimmy is always so sweet to his employee's.
I guess that's the reason they made him President of the Jaycees.
Even though he is unorganized, they still call him the Rib King.
He has two locations in Hagerstown where he can be seen
When growing up I heard he had a stuffed animal named "Percy"
I believe when a child he was at everyone's mercy.
Someone told me his parents were Nancy and Bill.
I bet they helped him up many long hills.
His brothers and sisters were Tommy, Becky, and Craig.
When he was younger, I wonder if they ever made him beg.
Jimmy loves to drink Diet Pepsi and eat penny candy
He's very forgetful and messy but he is still handy.
To my surprise he got married to Claire.
People came to see the wedding, the blessings filled the air
Now they both ride all over the countryside on his bike.
I wonder when the two of them will have a little tyke.
He rides over the four-state area in his Rodeo and his Jeep.
Trying to forget about his budget every day of the week.
He loved to help others when he was a child.
Now has the same qualities for others he's walk a mile.

1-19-98

44

John Allen Scott

Mr. Scott was the teacher in homeroom
He used a paddle but had no broom.
Lived with Evelyn and son, up Gardner Road
In spring and summer the grass they mowed.
He was the teacher for Vo.Ag. and for Shop.
If you talk to his students, he was at the top.
He always did F.F.A. with them in the summer
But he did not get around in any hummer.
He traveled to many of his boys homes
Never did he get lost or did he ever roam.
Mr. Scott and three of his boys went to Oklahoma City to judge
The National land Judging Contest and they did not budge.
He also taught his boys to dip sheep
To be a hard worker and friendships to keep.
He would get side tracked in class and tell stories of war
Got wild hairs out of my eye that made it very sore.
He wore a camera around his neck most of the time
Had honeybees and sold honey that cost more than a dime.
At lunchtime the Vo. Ag. Boys would pop corn to sell
In your homeroom or hallway there was a good smell.
They made copies of pictures that they took
In a file cabinet in school was their scrapbook.
He took his boys on camping trips overnight
Guided his students so they would turn out right.
Mr. Scott was a very dedicated person to his class
His goal was for his boys to learn, not just pass.
He was a good impact on all his boys
They had lots of fun and many joys.

5-31-2005

Jonathan

There once was a little boy I know.
Who loved to go sledding in the snow.
His favorite food was wheat bread and honey.
But it cost his parents a lot of money.
He has a brother Timmy & sisters Elizabeth & Amy Joy,
They all share the same house and even the toys.
Jonathan loves to tell people about his jokes.
But Elizabeth would rather be drinking coke.
When he grows up he wants to sell things.
I guess he's thinking of all the money it will bring.
Jonathan writes letters to all of his pen pals.
Which is a lot more interesting, than looking at an owl.
His favorite pastime is going on visitation on the van.
All over the city and town with Dad and Mr. Dan.
His mother Elaine teaches him at home schooling.
Now Jonathan will have a better chance not to roam.
Well this is not the end of my little story.
Cause Jonathan's not growed up but he's on his way to glory.

1-15-98

Mildred

Mildred is my best friend's mother.
She has one sister and two brothers.
She rides the commuter bus to town.
Often in the stores she can be found.
Unusually different as you can see.
Quick and sharp and busy as a bee.
She has to have her candy bars and Yoo-hoos.
I don't know how she wears those high hill shoes.
Crawls around on the floor with little Ruthann.
Next thing we hear, she'll be playing in the sand.
Can crochet all kinds of pretty things.
And loves to hear the humming birds sing.
Always climbs out on the house.
But would you believe, she's afraid of a mouse.
Her favorite pastime is taking a little nap.
She can sleep anywhere, even on a map.
Her family is the center of her life.
To spend time with them is not any strife.
When she comes to church she's always cold.
But one thing about it, she is very bold.

3-24-98

Miss Scott

In High School Miss Scott was my teacher
If we tried, most everyone could reach her.
She instilled in me to enjoy, to read books
I'd go to the library and look and look.
She was our homeroom teacher for a time
Could talk to you and make things rhyme.
When in school, she was very special to me
Taught our English class and made it easy to see.
In later years, she taught at Athens College
She was very smart and had lots of knowledge.
At home she likes to work in her garden
But those pesky bugs, she does not pardon.
As the years go by, we send cards
Keeping in touch for us wasn't very hard.
She goes to Bible study with her friends
They talk of God and all he sends.
Remained single and has never married
Keeps herself busy and she never tarried.
Lived in Athens most of her life
Surely along the way, she had some strife.
Miss Scott was very close to her mother
Had no sisters and only four brothers.
Well time has passed and she's older now
Still on many topics, she can tell you how.
She hasn't changed much but now has gray hair
But if she's your friend she will always care.

5-30-2005

Nancy

Several years ago God gave me a very special friend.
She is a sweet person on whom I can depend.
We've gone to the same church for many years.
And have been there for each other thru heartache and tears.
We both enjoy doing the very same thing.
Teaching boys and girls about Jesus and how to sing.
She loves working in the yard with her flowers.
There is where she could spend many long hours.
Has grandchildren Rebekah, Stephen and Ruthann.
To have more I know is part of her plan.
Her pride and joy are her children Dan and Sue.
To see them serve the Lord is a dream come true.
Nancy sure does have the prettiest yellow roses.
Always sharing and giving to others a little posy.
She loves cooking for her family Sunday lunch.
Sometime when they sit down, it's quite a bunch.
I've had friends that come and went.
Lots of time and energy with them I've spent.
But only one friend has come and stayed.
And for me everyday I know she prayed.

1-18-98

Ruthann

Ruthann is Dan and Rayanna's first child.
With her they have traveled many miles.
She has filled their life with lots of fun.
As the days go by there's more to come.
Loves to look at pictures of her friends.
But wears her diapers without any pins.
She always makes this funny little face,
At home or church or just any place.
In a few days Ruthann will be 1 year old.
And is cutting teeth and has a cold.
I love to watch her eat her lunch.
With her family and the rest of the bunch,
At church she loves to shake hands.
Even though there's not very many fans.
Ruthann brings fun to all she meets.
She likes to ride on all the streets.
My prayer for Ruthann will be,
When old enough, to be saved eternally.

7-21-98

Virginia & Robert

I have two friends named Virginia and Robert.
When we first met they lived at Greenside.
Robert loved to go fishing near the tide.
We would always go for our country walks.
I'd pick on Robert and Virginia and me would talk.
We'd ride the commuter bus to the Valley Mall.
And hope and pray none of us would fall.
On Thursdays was always their church night.
They would go with friends and family in sight.
Now they live at the Potomac Towers.
Poor Virginia has no place to plant her flowers.
In just a few years things have changed for them.
They can't ride the bus, its too much fuss for him.
In her old age Virginia now has a bird.
It's the silliest bird I ever heard.
They are two of the sweetest people you'll ever meet.
Virginia is Pete and Robert is Repeat.
They are my friends as you can see.
Come follow me, you'll be busy as a bee.

8-6-98

Humor

Cookout

The Fourth of July is a day for family cookouts.
There are usually happy people and very few pouts.
Come one, come all. Bring your burgers and friends
Be sure to invite the cook on whom you can depend.
Where's the chili and onions for the dog on the bun?
So we can eat while still on the run.
Chips and pretzels, snacks all around.
Be very careful or you'll gain a few pounds.
Last comes dessert, cakes, pies, are all on the table.
So come join our fun if you are still able.

7-3-01

Feet

God gives us two feet to get around
Then helps to keep them firmly on the ground.
Most people are born with ten little toes
Five on each foot all straight in a row.
We use our feet to walk and even to run
And stretch them out when lying in the sun.
You have twenty-eight bones in your feet
When older, it's easy to break them in the street.
If you don't keep them clean, they will stink
Sometimes the foot doctor marks them with ink.
Feet can cause you trouble, as you go along
You get hammer- toes, bunions, spurs, but no song.
Next, come fallen arches and swollen feet
Joint pain so severe you're searching for the heat.
You may even have to have foot surgery
Friends stop by and a member of the clergy.
We are told to wrap with CO-Flex and to elevate
How we wish for a pedicure and to celebrate.
If you're lucky, you won't have corns or a cyst
Could end up in a cast or fall and break your wrist.
Most likely you'll get special shoes to wear
Finding the right pair, you could pull your hair.
Most important, remember God gave you two
So use them to live for Him and be true.

6-4-20

Hair

Most people are born with plenty of hair.
They leave this Old World as bald as a pear.
Never happy with what God has given them.
They try everything with those bobbie pins.
First we straighten and then we curl.
Next we turn around and twirl.
The cycle goes on now we braid.
If we could we sure would trade.
I guess I'll try it up in a bun.
It will help when I'm on the run.
Well I'm too busy, I'll wear it straight.
Now with a little help I won't be late.
Oh, my color makes me look too old.
Should I change it and be bold?
Time has passed and I'm turning gray.
I'll have to find some other way.
So now, I will be happy as can be.
And thank God for the way he made me.

5-13-99

Knee Replacement

Exercise, Exercise, do your very best.
Or you'll fail the going home test.
Down to the parlor we will go.
Pushing out walkers in a row.
Now you'll sit on firm, straight back chairs.
Well at least you can still comb your hair
No sitting on the bottom of the tub.
Just stand on the floor and rub, rub, rub.
Getting dressed will surely be a chore.
For your poor ole knee will be sore.
But keep the faith, you'll be very well soon.
And you will go singing a new tune.
So you see, work is the name of the game.
To one day greatly ridding your pain.
We thank God for our doctors who have such skills.
It's a whole lot better than taking arthritic pills.

7-2-01

Old Age

If we live, old age comes to one and all.
No matter how big you are or how small.
We are born into this world with fingers and toes.
They are all lined up strait in a row.
We also have eyes, ears and a nose.
To hear the birds, to see and smell the rose.
God gives us hair for a covering for our head.
It can be styled many ways and messed up when you go to bed.
They say getting older sure in no fun.
But I know it can still keep you on the run.
When you get older you start loosing your teeth.
No matter how much you brush and floss a week.
You get wrinkles and brown spots all over you.
No matter how hard you look you can't find a decent shoe.
Your hair turns gray and falls out all over the place.
You wonder if it is going to be a hairless race.
And if that is not enough, we forget who we are.
We can't half remember when strangers talk to us.
When they come to our home or we meet on the bus.
There is a blessing to old age like none other.
God gives us grandchildren to love and to hold.
So even tho I've told you a lot, there is more to be told.
So why not go ahead and enjoy life and be bold not old.

3-22-03

Waiting

When we are conceived, our parents wait for the day.
To have a healthy boy or girl to come their way.
As the days go by, they wait for you on your own to eat.
Learn how to walk and not hurt your little feet.
They wait for you to get your mouth full of teeth.
Family stands by and looks at them in unbelief.
Soon you are in school and they wait for the bus
They pray you have made friends you can trust.
Next you wait and dread those hard teenage years.
At the very best, you will shed many tears.
Now they have grown up and left the nest.
You wait for their next visit and take a rest.
You wait when you ride the bus to go to town.
Most anywhere in the area, you can be found.
When you go to the doctor, you also have to wait
If you were younger, maybe you would skate.
Your wait is over and now you wait for test results to come in.
So you see, we spend a lot of time waiting down here
We loose our loved ones and cry many tears
The most important wait is for Jesus to return.
To go to your heavenly home, how your heart yearns.

6-30-2005

Nature

Bunny

A big bunny came hopping down the road.
He had two ears and a tiny pink nose.
He said, would you like me on your table?
Come catch me then, if you're able.
I sure would make a delicious meal,
For someone whose quick on their heels.
Do you think you could handle the job?
I know I'd taste better than that old cob.
So on he ran and scampered away.
And no one has seen him until today.
He was right, he sure tasted good.
Now he never runs through the woods.

5-7-99

Clouds

God uses clouds in many different ways.
To perform his wonders from day to day.
The clouds bring us rain sleet and snow.
And ushers in the mighty wind that blows.
They look like big fluffy pillows of cotton
That God places up in the beautiful sky.
They are so pleasant and soothing to the eye.
And are so awesome they should not be forgotten.
The clouds are the dust of his feet.
To see them would be something really neat.
He has blotted out our sins as a thick cloud.
How I praise and thank him out loud.
Out of the cloud God spoke to man.
And while he listened, God gave his command.
God used a cloud to guide and defend his people.
They had a tabernacle to worship in but no steeple.
When he established the clouds above,
Jesus was beside him with much love.
Even unto the clouds his faithfulness reaches.
In his word his strength and truth it teaches.
His covering was the thick clouds of the skies.
One day He is coming and I shall see him with my eyes.
The day of the Lord is near, a cloudy day
Will you be ready? Or will you stay?

12-27-03

Deer

Deer are very beautifully made
To hunt them, people have even paid.
God the creator formed them all
Some are short, some are tall.
Their heads are in many homes
Where they will never more roam.
They're killed every year for food
Tho some think it's very rude.
Two jumped off the railroad track
Made a mess and broke their back.
They often run into people's cars
Do damage and leave emotional scars.
I've had many experiences with deer
They caused my husband to shed many tears.
So, if you love deer, you're not alone.
There're many others just like you
Who would rather see them at the zoo.

5-17-05

The Groundhog

He gets up early and puts out his head
Usually when you are lying in bed.
Lives mostly underground or under homes
He may even find one of your combs.
He has long teeth and a short tail.
Let him bite you and you will wail.
If you watch them, it can be fun
But if they see you, they will run.
It sure is nice to watch them play
They scamper around most everyday.
They love to lay flat on their stomach to rest
I've never seen one make him self a nest.
They are destructive little creatures
Could irritate most any preacher.
Someone said they like vanilla wafers to eat
Most people agree with them, it is a nice treat.
On Feb 2nd they are used to forecast the weather
Snowflakes are falling and they look like a feather.
When they are small, they make a good pet
But you can't keep them in with only a net.
If you need to know more, you can find out the rest
Because, they sure can be a nuisance and a pest.

5-24-05

Mice

You wonder why, God created the mice
Because no one thinks they are very nice.
But they have a reason for being here
If only to scare some people to tears
They get into your food leave messes behind
Into the cereal boxes whatever they can find.
People scream when they run across the room.
They throw shoes or hit them with a broom.
As an animal they are pretty quiet
But can disturb your sleep and cause a riot.
I think they are kind a cute when small
Someone dropped one from a building and let it fall.
We bait the trap with all kinds of cheese
He gets away and says, "try again please"
God did make one who likes the mice
The lonely cat, and for him, they are very nice.

8-23-05

Red Bird

God made you to fly in the sky.
You are so beautiful to my eye.
Of all the birds that fly around,
You're the prettiest that can be found.
There are many birds up in the trees.
They fly around with every breeze.
But none is arrayed in such beauty.
To take care of them is our duty.
You fly everywhere with your coat of red.
And secretly listen to what is said.
But you're my favorite as you see,
Cause you've made a collector out of me.

1-24-98

Spiritual

A Missionary

God calls missionaries far and wide.
To serve him in other countries and abide.
Some on land and some on sea.
Wherever they go, it's the same earnest plea.
They leave home, family and friends behind.
Knowing they can trust God in their mind.
Sent out to live by faith in God to undertake.
Trusting him alone because he makes no mistake.
Great is their task and time is running short.
For they will soon meet their maker to report.
Many have been martyred for their faith in God.
Yet he still sends others, to walk the path they trod.
Paul and Barnabas were the first missionaries to be sent.
They preached in many lands and time was well spent.
In many places whole cities came to hear them preach.
God in his mercy gave them a large outreach.
In some countries the people are hungry for Gods word.
It's the most precious and sweetest story they have heard.
God sends many blessings all along the way.
As they strive to serve him from day to day.
So if you are call to be a missionary. Don't delay!
For God will help you all along the way.

11-10-03

Amazing Grace

Amazing grace was given to me
When to God, I called on bended knee.
God drew me with his cords of love and I was found.
Where sin abounded, Grace did much more abound.
I'll live for him with all my might.
That I may find grace in his sight.
We are not under law but grace.
All is commanded to run the race.
We are freely justified by his grace
Grace to you and peace from God our Father.
I can talk to him anytime, it's no bother.
And we beheld his glory, full of grace and truth.
Oh, how I love the story of Ruth.
The Lord will give you grace and glory.
His is the most wonderful story.
Tells us to sing with grace in our hearts.
And always let iniquities depart.
For by the grace of God, I am what I am.
Into this grace where in we stand.
For by grace are ye saved through faith.

11-8-03

Angels

We are told about angels in God's word.
No one on earth has seen or even heard.
God sends us his angels from all around.
Wherever his children can be found.
They're our heavenly messengers from above.
They come our way with much love.
He gives his angels charge over your care.
Then uses angels to bring answers to your prayers.
Let all the angels of God worship him.
Many books have been written about them.
God gives guardian angels to all his own.
No matter where you live or are known.
Angel of the Lord encamped about them that fear him.
They will be as close to you as any friend.
When its time for your soul to take its flight.
Angels will carry you way out of sight.
One day from heaven Jesus will come for his own.
With his mighty angels to welcome his children home.

11-25-03

Blessed Children

Children are a heritage from above.
They are given for us to love.
If we listen to God and obey
He will help us in every way.
Suffer little children to come unto me
Teach them to love me upon your knee.
Even a child is known by his ways.
With Jesus in his heart, he'll be happy all his days.
Train up a child in the way he should go
And when he is old he will not depart.
In the fear of the Lord is strong confidence
His children shall have a place of refuge.
Blessed is the man, Blessed is the man
Blessed is the man whom God gives.
Blessed is the man, Blessed is the man
Blessed is the man whom God gives children

7-18-97

Encouragement

When everything around me seems to fall apart.
I will trust in God, with all my heart.
I will not be discouraged, Jesus is my friend.
Whatever happens to me, on him I can depend.
He feeds the sparrow, and clothes the lilies in the field.
Why then should I fret and have to take a pill.
God knows all that will befall me in everyday.
And I know God in his wisdom has made for me a way.
I will pray for strength and help from God on high.
And never question his reasons for he knows the why.
Fear not I am with thee, Oh be not dismayed
For I am thy God and will still give thee aid.
So I will be like David and be encouraged in the word.
And he will take care of me, as he does the little bird.

4-6-01

God's Love

God's love is shed abroad in our hearts through his word.
His love reaches out to everyone all over the whole world.
It's not important where you're from or who you are.
His love reaches the farthest star.
No matter how wicked you've been,
His love covers all your sin.
God is the only one who loves us at all times.
His concern is for the lost one, so he leaves the ninety and nine.
He commands us to love one another, as he has loved us.
His love is seeking and calling us when we don't trust.
God's love suffereth long, is kind and never pushed on you.
It passes all knowledge; it beareth and endureth all things.
Greater love hath no man, so having not seen we love him.

11-19-98

God Will Provide

You gave your life to follow his call
Knowing Satan would tempt you to fall.
God has promised to guide you all the way
If close by his side, you always stay.
Greater is he that is in you, than in the world
Tho many things at you may be hurled.
Any weapon against God's servants shall fail
Because they come from the pit of Hell.
As you run this race, trials make you grow
If you live your life and let your light glow.
Things always seem brighter the next day
When we come to God and unceasingly pray.
Our victory is only complete in Him
When totally on Him we depend.
So whatever may happen, whatever betide,
God has promised to always be by your side.

1-28-05

God's Word

God's word was given to sinful man.
To teach him how to live a godly life.
His word says to build on the rock, not on the sand.
You'll have joy unspeakable and a lot less strife.
We are commanded to memorize God's word.
There are millions who have never heard.
We are told to bind God's word upon our fingers
You can listen to it through dedicated singers.
We are to hide his word in our hearts
To live a life for him and never depart.
God's word is a lamp unto our feet.
It lights our way all over the streets.
Length of days you'll have, if His word you keep
His eyes ever behold thee, for he does not sleep.
Every word of God is pure His word is truth.
You can read it in the story of Ruth.
God gives us his power to speak His word
When it goes forth, it's not always heard.
The law of the Lord is perfect, converting the soul
It blesses your heart and it makes you whole.
God's word can even melt the heart of stone
You find a new family and you are not alone.
God's word has stood the test of time
I'm so glad I'm his and He is mine.
God's word shall never ever pass away
When he gave his word, it's here to stay.
Add thou not unto His word, lest he repose thee.
He gave his life for you, for all to see.
In the beginning was the Word
The Word was with God and the Word was God.

5-25-05

Heaven

God made Heaven, earth and the sea.
For his created being you and me.
He gave his son on the cruel cross.
So you and I will not be lost.
Inherit the kingdom prepared for you.
Up in the sky, beyond the blue.
In heaven God's glory will be revealed in us.
For those who have given him total trust.
A Holy City that is built foursquare.
For the redeemed who are going there.
I've heard some people say it's Paradise.
But they've never seen it with their eyes.
Described as a house in Gods Word.
Millions over the world have never heard.
In heaven he worketh signs and wonders.
He sends the storms and the thunder.
Heaven of heavens cannot contain him.
So let your light shine and not grow dim.
An inheritance reserved in heaven for you.
If you live for Him and remain true.
In heaven there will be no more tears or heartache.
Build up your treasure in heaven that won't break.
Tell others about Jesus and be very bold.
Then one day you'll walk on streets of gold.
He is coming in the clouds for me.
Of this I am assured I have the victory.
In heaven my name is written down
O how I long to hear the trumpet sound.
In heaven God is sitting on his throne.
To welcome all his children home.

4-25-99

I Am Going to a City

I am going to a city that is built foursquare.
Jesus is my pilot, he's taking me there.
I will be free from all pain.
That on earth I must bear.
For Jesus takes all my cares
So give your life to him and be free from sin.
If you searched the world you'd find no better friend.
He'll give you peace within your heart.
That will never more depart.
Let Jesus take all your cares.
Yes, Jesus is taking me there.
Nothing in the world can be compare
He's the only way to live day by day.
Won't your let Jesus take your there?

4-27-99

Jesus

While traveling through life one day.
I heard a total stranger say.
His name is the Ancient of Days.
He's helped others in many ways.
He'll take your load of sin today.
And cast it all very far away.
He bled on the cross for the human race.
Up Calvary's mountain, he took your place.
I listened to this man as he talked.
For with Jesus I knew he walked.
The Rose of Sharon is his name.
To save lost sinners was why he came.
Life eternal he promises to you.
If for him your life remains true.
He's Lord and Savior of us all.
When upon his name we call.
He said Jesus is the Hope of Glory.
A Friend of Sinners is his story.
Known as the Only Wise God
Many miles for others he trod.
Lily of the Valley, The Bright and Morning Star,
People came to hear his wisdom from afar.
The King of Glory and The Living Bread,
His words are the most often read.
My High Tower in the midst of storm.
To shield and protect me from all harm.
Mighty Deliver of the whole world.
When Satan's darts at us are hurled.
For me he is The Precious Cornerstone.
Yet in his death, he died alone.
Many have tried The Lord of Hosts.

Found in Jesus only they could boast.
A very Righteous Judge to you he'll be.
When on the day of reckoning you'll see.
He's the Almighty, The Beginning and The End.
Please trust in him, he'll be your dearest friend.

1-23-98

My Victory is Complete

When I reach the other side, O what glory that will be.
I'll see Jesus, the one who gave his life for me
Thank him for amazing grace and for taking my place
He saved my soul, O bless his precious name
When I reach the other side, heavenly angels will be there
Singing praises day and night around God's throne.
O what sweet communion there nothing else can compare
To be in God's presence through out all eternity
When I reach the other side. What a day that will be.
I'll see my mother whose there waiting for me.
Glad hosanna's we will sing to Jesus our King.
He reigns forever, O bless his holy name.
My Victory is complete, My Victory is complete.
They nailed his hands and his feet.
My Victory is complete.

5-17-99

Prayer

Prayer is pouring your heart out to God.
Nothing else can ever compare
Telling him all you could never share.
God is never too busy to listen to you
Whether you're happy, sad or blue.
It doesn't even cost you a dime,
If you're faithful, just your time
Sweet fellowship that will be,
When you talk to God on bended knee.
It's such a blessing just to pray
Doesn't matter how long you stay.
God is still faithful to his word.
Keep your heart clean and you will be heard.
Bring your burdens. God will make a way.
If you come and unceasingly pray
If we pray according to Gods will.
Then sit and listen and be very still
God will hear as in days of old
In God's word the stories are told.
Daniel prayed morning, night and noon.
He believed Jesus could come very soon.
So whatever your problem or your need
Go to God and beg and plead.

5-18-05

Sickness

I've suffered so in this world below.
Only God my dearest friend knows.
One day to Heaven my soul will go.
Sickness and sorrow I'll not know.
Years of pain and agony will vanish away.
When he calls me home to stay.
All tears will be forever gone.
For I am in my heavenly home.
To be with Jesus who died for me.
How I long his dear face to see.
I'll spend eternity on high.
Up in the Sweet Bye and Bye.
Sweet communion we'll have up there.
Nothing else on earth could compare.
So you see it's not the end my friend.
My new life with Jesus is about to begin.
So I will enjoy the trip and the view,
Because everything will be brand new.

11-8-03

Thanks

It is such a little word to say.
When you are taken care of day by day.
The word is little but the results are big
It makes you happy, even if you're in a rig.
Doesn't take too much time to say thank you.
Can be the difference between sad and being blue.
Jesus gave us the example in His word.
Millions have read the stories and have heard.
He always gave thanks before he ate
For whatever was received on his plate.
One leper gave thanks, when he came.
He was healed, changed and no longer the same.
Give thanks unto God, for he is good.
We should always thank him for our daily food.
Forever thank him for the blessings of each day.
Pray a grateful person you will always stay.

8-23-05

The Cross

Jesus died on the old rugged Cross.
He took our place at an awful cost.
He suffered such pain and agony
To show his love for you and me
No greater love has ever been shown.
To provide for you an eternal home,
His love still beckons and calls today.
Through Christ Jesus is the only way.
A home up in heaven is prepared for you.
Up in the sky way beyond the blue
So come to the cross and not delay.
For on earth you'll find no better way.

11-13-03

The Holy Spirit

The Holy Spirit came as a mighty rushing wind
He fills the believers and those he sends.
When you believe in God and are saved
The Holy Spirit convicts you on how you behave.
If obedient to his leading, He will teach you
He indwells and guides you, if you are true.
Walks along beside you wherever he may send
Will be your Comforter when you lose your friend.
Gives discernment when you read His precious Word.
Helps you to tell others who have never heard.
He gives you the spiritual gifts to serve God
Will never leave you wherever you may trod.
Sends out missionaries far and wide
There is nowhere from His presence we can hide.
He empowers the believers to do His task
Nothing is too hard that H would ask.
You can quench The Holy Spirit and grieve
But God's blessing, you will not receive.
Helps our infirmities when we are not well
Anoints and sanctifies us His stories to tell.
The Holy Spirit will bear fruit in your life
He will bring joy and peace, but never strife.
The Holy Spirit strives with the sinner to repent and turn
If not, one day he will go to Hell and forever burn.

6-8-2005

The Only One

I searched for fame down here but all in vain.
Nothing I did would bring me peace.
Then one day a friend of mine came to spend a little time.
She told me of one who heals all hearts.
On earth there is one who knows my deepest woes.
I go to him each day in prayer.
He sees me on bended knee.
And He hears my every plea.
Without him how lost I would be.
Now Jesus walks with me through every valley.
He's my dearest friend on him I can depend.
He leads and guides me peace in every way.
And will take me to Heaven with him one day.
Could I introduce you to the Only One?
His arms are wide open to welcome you home.
You'll find peace and comfort in his loving arms.
His name is Jesus, for He's the Only One.

7-13-97

Worry

From the time we are old enough we all worry.
Whether it is in leisure or in a hurry.
We worry, if we'll have friends in school
There is a tried and proven rule.
A friend must show himself a friend to be
Go on with life "don't worry" all will see.
We worry if we'll find the right one to date
We cry and spend sleepless nights as we wait.
When we worry, it can choke out God's word.
Things become more important, than what we've heard.
God has promised to meet all our needs
If we trust in him and humbly plead.
He has promised to protect all his own.
Wherever you may be or choose to roam.
Be careful for nothing let your needs be known unto him.
Don't worry, he has promised to be with you to the end.
So why worry? When you can pray.
Live for God and close by his side always stay.

8-23-05

You

You are my Savior and my friend.
You gave your son, for all my sin.
You gave me salvation, full and free.
You died for everyone, as they can see.
You sent your Holy Spirit to be our guide
From you there is nowhere we can hide.
If we listen, he guides us everyday.
When he came he's here to stay.
You will always be my hiding place
Help me to always stay in the race.
You pick me up, when I fall down
You set my feet on solid ground.
You are my helper and my shield
Help me never to be afraid to yield.
Without you, I'd have no hope or strength
I'm so happy your love has no length.
You became my Redeemer and my King
It is so wonderful of you to sing.
So I will give you my all in all
And daily on you continue to call.
For there is no life without you
Because you are my rock, and this is true.

5-23-05

Printed in the United States
52243LVS00006BA/180